Tending My Piece of the World Garden

by Daisy Fields

Copyright © 2022 by Daisy Fields

All rights reserved

ISBN 978-1-62806-351-6 (print | paperback)

Library of Congress Control Number 2022906539

Salt Water Media
29 Broad Street, Suite 104
Berlin, MD 21811
www.saltwatermedia.com

Cover image by the author

Interior photographs by the author;
illustration of the daisy by Jim Adcock

For my family and friends,
for keeping me aware of the importance
of tending your own spiritual garden
and each other's.

To the one holding this:
Read these words
Tuck flowers in between
Dogear the pages
Doodle while you daydream
Underline your favorites
Color in the blooms
Add your own designs
Take it along with you

I met someone today
Who opened a window for me
I saw a kite fly by
And grabbing its tail
I wondered where it shall lead
I know it will set me free

If rain were to fall right now
To let it cover and soak my skin
I will wait for thunder and lightning
If only to drink it in
With eyes open as puddles surround
Everything is lifted
And roots grow into the ground

Sun warms the skin
An adventure begins
You are the one
Who can make it become
A beautiful day
Not a worry to say
A smile will guide
It's you who decides
The difference between
Peace and stress

Do I try too hard
To keep the past gone
To be someone new
To hide what is true
And be what I think
I should be

What would I change
If I could do it again
To ask for a kiss
And not speak
With no promises to say
I long for the day
At last no work
And all play

I give this to you
My wonderful muse
who inspired me to pick up my pen
a beautiful day
quiet, on the bay
I miss you
My dear, dear friend

Afraid to walk away
If it starts
Will it stay?
Or will it be gone again.
A necessary outlet
A selfish project
I need it either way

Blow in the breeze
With the lightness of air
Where will it carry
What will be there
Can't fight the direction
It has in mind
Go with the wind
See what you find

Such a nice conversation
Of a time, that's passed
Most things don't
But some they do last
Why is it fear
Can cost us the most
Who spends their life
Love/hating a ghost
Illusions are a trap
Open your eyes
Reality is there
NOW is paradise

Don't try so hard
To make things be
Don't miss a chance
To see what's to see
Leaves changing color
A chill in the breeze
The flight of a bird
The absence of a bee
Beauty in this world
Not goals in a row
A storm on the horizon
Can distract from the rainbow

A spirit floats
Just waiting to be born
So, she can forget
Most everything she's learned
Only to see
If she can remember it again

Above the latter blend
of the day and pen
Enjoy the moment
And own it

I gave willingly
You took everything you could
I am stopping now

Life is darkness and light
A wounded bird takes flight
It hides from the cold
Hopes one day to grow old
And no longer have to fight

High tide low
Low tide high
Country road
Open sky
Here come the geese
Riding the water
Nothing is as valuable
As wholehearted laughter

Maybe it's under this flower

I'll look and I'll see
I'll find what it means
The petals, the seeds
The beauty in between
The seconds, the minutes
The hours

There are many truths
Yours, mine, the ghosts
We hold tightly to our own
Experiences and observations grow
So, our truth begins
We spread it ahead and
Leave it where we've been
To be open to each moment
The hear and then the now
The practice of our lifetime
A journey of the soul

Money allows space
For falseness
Cushions illusions
Buffers the pain
Falseness begins
The distance
The beginning
of the end
Who is this person anyway?
Causing damage
While whispering
Friend

A dream can
Be large or small
It can be so loud
It takes over
who you are
so quiet that
no one knows
it's there
What is your dream?
Is it shaped like everywhere?
A circle or star
Is it right where you are?
Bursting in flames
Burned and charred
Or clean and pristine
Hey, it's your dream.

Much control is hidden
In compliments and gifts
You must let it go
Fly away
Be set free
Put it down
Leave it here
Stop carrying
Be yourself
Bloom anew
Say goodbye
Let it die
Close your eyes
Not listen
Look within
Become Zen

Whenever it is
That I wonder what's the point
I watch a flower

You talk like it's a fault
but it's really your opinion
these are not facts
they are not freeing

I want to help you
But I don't know who you are
I know you are hurting
I want to let you know
It is not your fault

It seems so easy to disappoint
To not live up to expectations
But it's hard to accept
That you've failed
Despite your dedication
Once you see
That it happens readily
And there's nothing
That one can do
Except to go on
And on and on
Together we are alone

I happily implore
My dreams from before
My need to explore
Help me to walk out the door
I freely express
My need for excess
Freedom to bless
The world with my presents
I wonder aloud
As my thoughts come about
With no expectations or doubt
Just the freedom to fall out

Ocean wash my soul
Wash and scrub it clean
Leave my fears behind me
Sink them to the deep
They are useless to me now
I've more important things to keep

I'm not just here to be pleasing
To the eye and ear
What about you?
Why are you here?

The good times pass so quickly
And the bad go on and on

What is up with this world
Its people are strange
They run like hamsters on a wheel
Chasing a future,
they've doomed in their mind to fail
Doing unhealthy things just to feel
Wasting resources
Throwing away time
Missing the moments
Like its justified
Standing their ground
On a mountain they hate
Proving that life
Is full of mistakes

The water overtakes the sand
It cleanses the space
Clears an area for understanding
Makes time for a break
For a minute
One lets go
For a moment
One forgets
It doesn't matter who wins
No one cares what's next

The waters always moving
Seeking its level
Open to change
Not really trying to do better
The calming effect
It has on the soul
Is there when you need it
It's always at home

I wonder what the sun thinks
We say it burns too hot
What are the thoughts the ocean has?
The pollution we don't stop
The trees can't do their job
Though we have it figured out
The earth can see our arrogance
How does it choose to shout?

The earth accepts our weakness
Our excess and our waste
We treat it like our mother
With ignorance and distaste
We use it up and wear it out
Exhaust the inner spirit
We wonder why there isn't more
When we are the ones who used it

Feels Like Freedom

Time to yourself
Time on the run
Time to go get 'em
Get things done
You have a plan
You have the start
First steps are taken
Get on your mark
Start expanding your mind
Expanding your view
Expand the mindset
There's so much to do
It won't always go smoothly
Expectations are fantasy
Begin, start now,
You can make your reality

What to do with today
A beautiful display
Contains all possibilities
It's you who decides
What to do with these
Choices overrun
While direction shows its face
Never enough money
To ever stop the chase
That is not the truth
Only that that we've been fed
Constant reinforcement
The media in your head
Turn left and right
Look up to the sky
This is where true life is,
Here, in you and I

I want to lose track of time
To forget the things I don't need
I want to remember to breathe
Stop trying to achieve
Give myself time to grieve

If love destroys me
So be it
I can't think
Of a more worthy cause

I don't have the strength
To show you how or why
Only to do it myself

Every time you make it real
You do just that
Your questions are
Like touching a bubble

What lies underneath
The smooth exterior
What churns the water
What is there to fear
Reaching to the vision
The one that comes and goes
Whatever causes this illusion
Don't ever let it go

I want these things
To float away
My thoughts, my dreams today
I give them up to what will be
Though I'm no fan of delay

May you have too many good thinks
Just enough friends, fun times, cold drinks
Plenty of love and laughs in excess
Memories and plans
Help to get through the rest

The sun starts the day
What will it hold
Try to delay
When the sadness takes hold
Stay in this moment
Try not to relive the past
Change is necessary
Let your heart relax

Life is funny
The things you learn
The laughter and joy
The choices you burn
Time flying by
The sun going down
Do everything you can
We only get once around

What is love about
Turning your insides out
Upturning your life
Rolling the dice
Following your heart
opening to the doubt
No guarantees
Everyone can leave
Enjoying each day
Allows the moment to stay
Following the sun
lowing in the sky
love is in the heart
even saying goodbye

leaves will change
autumn will come
ready or not
let's move on
make space for
new things
clear out the old
it's winter before you know it
dark and cold

you can't make
someone love you
and you can't make
yourself love someone
you don't

I was having a dream
Tangled in something
I couldn't see and
Couldn't get free
That's you and me

We gained perspective
We lost the old ways
Starting all over
The one I still chase
We lost years together
We gained material things
Lost sight of what's important
Nothing left, no one wins

Open your eyes
To the time it takes
Let things escalate
Don't self-hate
Open your arms
To the love that surrounds
Don't let there be doubt
Let your heart bounce
Open your heart
To the possibility of could
Create art for the good
It's needed like food
Open your mind
To the ideas of others
Try to listen beyond the clutter
Combine and wonder

I watched a wave dance today
And crabs crawl the shore
The seasons changed
The beach has been cleaned
What is behind the next door

Autumn occurred to me the other day
I hadn't thought of it in a while
Was this a new breeze
blowing me a smile

Time passes slowly
While I wait for you
My heart pains
It calls your name
Where are you now?
I draw you in

Life exists in tiny places
In whose tiny space, are we?
We say that the small things
They don't feel
It's what we do to get by

But the bees disagree
Their doing has need
With out them
We lose everything

Fear is real
Of both good and bad
Feel what you do
Not what you should have
Time can change things
Dreams can come true
They look so different in reality
It can be scary when they do.

You can learn a lot
From culture shock
If you don't try to blend

Waves, continuous waves
Starting the day
Finding the space
Reminded of my small
Yet essential way
Helps me to stay
And to try again

When the sun fades
And the water turns to ink
Darkness falls
Space to dream, to think
A beauty comes
Peaceful night
Waves continue, proving life.

The birds do not wonder about tomorrow
They are not fretted with plans
Do they speak of where they are heading?
Do they offer solace to friends?
I've seen them miss their other half
Somehow, they know their babies too
Their lifetimes are so limited
Really nothing else to choose

What is it the ocean has
That contains such mystery
How is it it ebbs and flows
Seeming to overcome all things
So easily it takes its place
With acceptance to its deep
What are the secrets the ocean still keeps?

Music to my ears
Time and effort
Creative combination
Emotional connection
External vibration
Collective efflorescence
Mind is in the present
Beautiful feeling
Perceived meanings
Releasing like medicine

The earth cycles round
A blue sky to solid ground
Lighting up the day
Putting night away
Plants go to seed
Some go to sleep
Creative minds awaken
Spread inspiration

Index of First Lines

A dream can 32
A spirit floats 21
Above the latter blend 23
Afraid to walk away 16
Autumn occurred to me the other day 81
Blow in the breeze 18
Do I try too hard 13
Don't try so hard 20
Every time you make it real 60
Fear is real 85
Feels Like Freedom 53
High tide low 27
I don't have the strength 59
I gave willingly 24
I give this to you 15
I happily implore 40
I met someone today 9
I want these things 64
I want to help you 37
I want to lose track of time 56
I was having a dream 75
I watched a wave dance today 79
I wonder what the sun thinks 50

I'm not just here to be pleasing 43
If love destroys me 57
If rain were to fall right now 10
It seems so easy to disappoint 39
Leaves will change 72
Life exists in tiny places 84
Life is darkness and light 26
Life is funny 68
May you have too many good thinks 65
Maybe it's under this flower 28
Money allows space 31
Much control is hidden 33
Music to my ears 93
Ocean wash my soul 41
Open your eyes 78
Such a nice conversation 19
Sun warms the skin 11
The birds do not wonder about tomorrow 90
The earth accepts our weakness 51
The earth cycles round 94
The good times pass so quickly 45
The sun starts the day 67
The water overtakes the sand 47
The waters always moving 49
There are many truths 30

Time passes slowly 82
Waves, continuous waves 88
We gained perspective 77
What is it the ocean has 92
What is love about 70
What is up with this world 46
What lies underneath 62
What to do with today 54
What would I change 14
When the sun fades 89
Whenever it is 34
You can learn a lot 86
You can't make 73
You talk like it's a fault 36

www.ingramcontent.com/pod-product-compliance
Lightning Source LLC
Chambersburg PA
CBHW071236090426
42736CB00014B/3107